Children's Playhouses

Plans and Ideas

Schiffer Publishing Ltd®

4880 Lower Valley Road, Atglen, PA 19310 USA

Tina Skinner

Dedication

To Helen, who inspired. To Brandi, who helped.
To Craig, who will end up doing all the work entailed herein.

Library of Congress Cataloging-in-Publication Data
Skinner, Tina.
Children's playhouses : plans and ideas / Tina Skinner.
p. cm.
ISBN 0-7643-1416-5 (pbk.)
1. Children's playhouses. I. Title.
TH4967.S55 2001
728'.9--dc21
2001001243

Front cover:
Left: *Photo by Teena Albert/Courtesy of Barbara Butler*, top right: *Photograph by John Sanderson/Courtesy of Lilliput Play Homes*,
bottom right: *Courtesy of Lilliput Play Homes*
Back cover:
Photography by Terence Roberts/Courtesy of the Delaware Art Museum
Title page: *Courtesy of Katelyn's Kastles*

Designed by Bonnie M. Hensely
Type set in Kids/Korinna BT

ISBN: 0-7643-1416-5
Printed in China

Published by Schiffer Publishing Ltd.
4880 Lower Valley Road
Atglen, PA 19310
Phone: (610) 593-1777; Fax: (610) 593-2002
E-mail: Schifferbk@aol.com
Please visit our web site catalog at **www.schifferbooks.com**

In Europe, Schiffer books are distributed by Bushwood Books
6 Marksbury Avenue Kew Gardens
Surrey TW9 4JF England
Phone: 44 (0) 20-8392-8585; Fax: 44 (0) 20-8392-9876
E-mail: Bushwd@aol.com
Free postage in the UK. Europe: air mail at cost.

This book may be purchased from the publisher.
Include $3.95 for shipping. Please try your bookstore first.
We are always looking for people to write books on new and related subjects.
If you have an idea for a book please contact us at the Atglen, PA. address.
You may write for a free catalog.

Courtesy of Katelyn's Kastles

Contents

Introduction

A small child changes the whole world. That's what little Helen Claire did to mine. Suddenly I am focused on what I can best do for my child. In researching that, I hope this book will reach hundreds of parents and educators, in turn touching the lives of thousands of children.

I fervently believe in the importance of providing fertile ground for our children's imaginations. It is vital to get them outdoors and away from electronic media that does all the thinking for them; to put them in places where play is active and original. It isn't necessary for a playhouse to have finials and gingerbread trim, to have electricity or plumbing, or to have furnishings in the latest styles. These things are well and fine if you can afford them. In a pinch, however, a refrigerator box will serve a child's play needs as well, if not as permanently.

It's important to keep in perspective that children can color in the grayest of tree houses with overlays of imagined sails billowing in the wind, of imaginary friends arriving for a tea party, of horses tethered up outside and ready to ride, of delicious mud pies fresh from the oven. A playhouse is an important place where a child can invent their own world for a day, a new role to act out, a new environment that they adorn with the trappings of their own imaginations.

You don't have to teach a child how to play in a playhouse. Simply show them the door. Lynda Bontrager, grand matron of the family-run Custom Playhouses, says it's an astonishing introduction to watch. She takes playhouses to the Minnesota State Fair every year and watches as even the smallest children explore the miniature homes. "The first thing they do is open and close the doors and windows," she says.

Still, it's the parents who buy these homes. It's a nostalgic thing, according to Lilliput Mansions founder Steven Chernicky. "They remember having a playhouse, or playing in a friend's. They want their children to have that kind of fun," he said.

The demand for children's playhouses is astonishing, as the builders featured in this book will attest. Each builder was drawn into this world by the small children in his or her own life, and each has discovered a surprising demand for their product nationally. On the non-commercial side, two projects are profiled here that were undertaken for charity, both of which were enormously successful.

This book, I hope, will stimulate more work for worthy causes, houses for charitable causes, houses for play in children's hospitals. Most importantly, I hope this book will open doors to the imaginations of both children and parents, and stimulate play.

Courtesy of Storybook Playhouses

For Fun and Fundraising

A gallery of artfully designed projects for the Delaware Art Museum's Fun at Play gala and auction

A member's idea to create children's playhouses and potting sheds and auction them off during a fundraiser turned into a bonanza for the Delaware Art Museum.

Volunteers helped organize fourteen teams consisting of an architect, a builder, an interior designer, and a landscape designer to participate in "Art at Play," as they coined the fundraiser. These teams brainstormed and built away, and before it was all over, the quest for creative and functional playhouses and potting sheds had become quite competitive. This was all to the benefit of those who came to bid at a grand gala; so charmed were these philanthropic guests, that they spent over $175,000 on the fourteen houses, the most sought-after one going for $21,000.

Following are their creations, including the potting sheds and a pool house. A complete list of the design team and contact information is included in the resources section at the end of the book.

Photography by Terence Roberts/Courtesy of the Delaware Art Museum

Copper Folly. The designers were inspired by the Greeks when they sketched out this neoclassical design with an all-white exterior, Venetian windows, and a vibrant copper roof. Double doors open to display a whimsical paint job inside by decorator Ronal Fenstermacher, who included what may be the most fantasized-about furnishing—a hammock.

Photography by Terence Roberts/Courtesy of the Delaware Art Museum

The Golden Rectangle. This ultra-contemporary playhouse was based on the Golden Rectangle design, a mystical shape found in both abstract mathematics and nature (i.e. the nautilus shell). Brilliant colors of golden yellow, cobalt blue, and white highlight the design of this playhouse. The roof is clear and allows a flood of natural light to enter. Built-in shelves and seats and an area for hanging tools or toys is inside.

Photography by Terence Roberts/Courtesy of the Delaware Art Museum

Cabin Fever. This playhouse looks pretty straight-forward, but there are secrets inside! A hidden room on the right is accessible only if you know to push on the pivoting wall. There a concealed staircase leads to a wooden trap door with leather hinges, which opens to reveal attic space.

Photography by Terence Roberts/Courtesy of the Delaware Art Museum

Photography by Terence Roberts/Courtesy of the Delaware Art Museum

Chez La Tête. Sunny colors brighten this wooden playhouse. You enter down a path of painted paver stones and through a mouth-like front door; exit out the ear-shaped window. The other ear window has a swing dangling from it. The eye-shaped windows in the front have shades with painted eyelashes on them.

Photography by Terence Roberts/Courtesy of the Delaware Art Museum

Photography by Terence Roberts/Courtesy of the Delaware Art Museum

Cottage Caribe.
Everyone fell in love with this little number, where everything was slightly askew (notice how the two front windows are different in size and shape), and nothing went without a coat of colorful paint. This wacky playhouse is made completely of recycled materials and features a periscope chimney, a tipsy dormer window, front porch with an overhang, and a sign ready for the new owner's name. Out back is a tire swing that hangs from an outrigger ridge.

Photography by Terence Roberts/Courtesy of the Delaware Art Museum

Sitting Pretty. This playhouse/potting shed is an authentic handcrafted timber frame cottage. A rooftop observation deck is beautifully designed with attractive latticework. Window boxes and a trellis roof overhang add to the garden theme. Inside, antique furniture, flowerpots, and numerous green plants contribute to the beauty of this structure.

Photography by Terence Roberts/Courtesy of the Delaware Art Museum

Photography by Terence Roberts/Courtesy of the Delaware Art Museum

Land's End. This lovely Victorian beach house features an attached tower with windows on all four sides. A handsome front window crowned by a peaked cap pediment and underlined with a flowerbox looks out over a wonderful rock garden.

The Yacht Club. In classic Boat House Row style, this playhouse was inspired by the Victorian Gothic architecture found along the banks of the Schuylkill River in Philadelphia, Pennsylvania. It features a weathervane, double doors, double-hung windows with shutters, and a multilevel roof. The marine theme continues inside, where faux rope trims the windows.

Photography by Terence Roberts/Courtesy of the Delaware Art Museum

Kevin's Ketch. Another miniature boathouse, this one includes a dock for a front porch. Rope handrails line the dock and keep the boat from floating away. Various nautical accents, such as a brass ship's bell, life preserver, blue heron weathervane, wood pilings, and fishnet add to the seafaring motif. The exterior of the house is weathered barn-board with trim painted to highlight the roof. The interior has Spanish cedar flooring with mahogany cabinetry and countertop.

Photography by Terence Roberts/Courtesy of the Delaware Art Museum

Picture Perfect. This cozy retreat was made from all wood siding and solid cedar. A stone walkway leads to French glass doors underneath a trellis of painted green wood. Several windows allow for natural sunlight and serve as design elements. Inside are a tiled potting table with working sink, and plenty of space for plants, trees, and flowers.

La Gloriette. Designed to resemble a French garden cottage, this house could first be used by the children, then taken over by the adults after the kids have grown. The design team finished it off as a place in which to store tools and other garden equipment. The large front door is outfitted with antique wrought-iron hinges and latch. Inside are built-in shelves and cabinets. Note that a few other occupants might take refuge here – built-in bird boxes are under the eaves.

Photography by Terence Roberts/Courtesy of the Delaware Art Museum

Wooddale. This is a replica of the Wooddale Covered Bridge in Greenville, Delaware. It can be used as both a potting shed and/or poolside or patio bar. The trompe l'oeil painting of horses and riders on the front greets all who enter. On the back there is a picture of the hindquarters galloping away. Windows are on both sides and let lots of sunshine in. A working sink is inside along with lots of counter space for plants or pitchers of one's favorite summer beverage.

Photography by Terence Roberts/Courtesy of the Delaware Art Museum

New Directions. Made of renewable and durable materials, this potting shed looks similar to a miniature greenhouse and acts in much the same way. Attractive and functional, operable windows allow light and air to comfortably flow through. The many amenities of this potting shed include ample storage space for mulch, soils, tools and plants, a sink, and a built-in work table.

THE GARDEN SHED

Time and Again. This potting shed takes on classic Roman characteristics with a columned entrance overshadowed by a handsome pediment. Wooden "barn-like" doors are topped by transom windows. A special storage area was built on one side. The inside is furnished with a potter's bench, antique watering cans and tools, and flower pots.

19

Building to Help the Abused

First they helped disadvantaged children,
now we share the blueprints for a few fancy raffle prizes

The following projects were the result of an idea conceived by Bob Goodier, of Goodier Builders in Columbia, Maryland. In early 1996, he helped organize a team that included several other area builders along with materials suppliers Georgia-Pacific and Style Solutions™, and architect Cynthia Tauxe of Atlanta, Georgia.

Together they created a village of children's playhouses that were built and then transported to a local shopping mall and landscaped on site. The playhouses were on view for several weeks in the mall while Voices for Children, a court-appointed special advocate program, held a raffle. Proceeds from raffling off the playhouses netted $11,500 for the community organization. The money was used to recruit and train special advocates for abused and neglected children in Howard County, Maryland.

The concept had been used before, Goodier said, but in the past the playhouses had been much bigger. Some were 12 feet high and difficult to transport in and out of the mall. "People were saying 'I'll take a chance on the raffle, but what do I do with it if I win it?' Goodier said. So the playhouses had to get smaller. "They were more functional, easier to put on a truck."

Style Solutions™, Inc., provided the following plans for five delightful children's houses. Professionally drafted, these blueprints can provide precise instructions for creating your own backyard treasure, or simply a jumping off point.

Bank on it

Roof: Georgia-Pacific "Summit Series" Shingles, Color: Surf Blue or Dove Grey

Appliqué: Style Solutions™ "Appliqué" APL5X10; paint white

Pediment: Style Solutions™ Peaked sunburst window pediment PSWDH24X12; paint white

Dentil Moulding: Style Solutions™ "Dentil Moulding" MLD332; paint white

Window Mantels: Style Solutions™ "Flat Trim" FLT120 plus window moulding MLDWM180; paint white

Window and Door Casing: Style Solutions™ "Window Moulding" MLDWM180; paint· white

Pilasters: Style Solutions™ fluted pilaster with adjustable plinth block PIL5X108; paint white

Window Sill: Style Solutions™ chair rail MLD610; paint white

Siding, Interior walls and ceiling: 1/2" Georgia-Pacific ACBC plywood; paint light blue

Floor: ¾" Georgia-Pacific ACBC plywood; paint gray

Ridge Boards: 2x6

Muntins: ½" strips of wood or plastic; paint white

Column Capitals: 2x2; paint white

Corner Boards: 1x3; paint white

Skirt: 1x6; paint white

Glazing: Clear Plexiglas

Door: 3/4" ACBC plywood, exterior grade; paint white with dark blue lettering, no astragal, magnet catch set in clear Plexiglas for windows, cabinet pull

Floor: Joists: 2x6 pressure treated wood at 12" on center

Rim Joists: 2x10 pressure treated wood

Skirt: 1x6; paint gray

Studs: 2x4s

Interior ceiling moulding, 1x6, Style Solutions™ MLD248-16

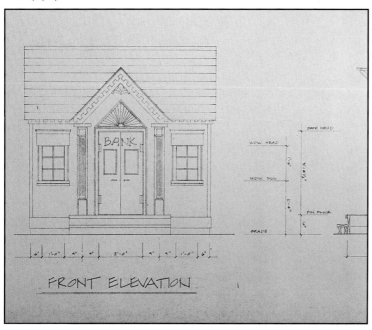

FRONT ELEVATION

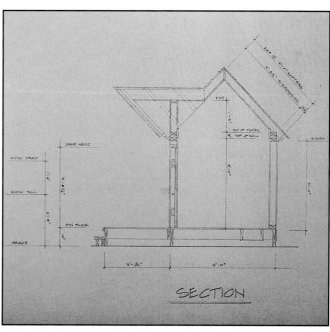

SECTION

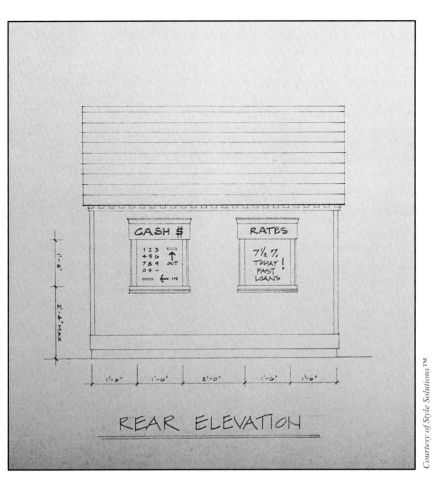

REAR ELEVATION

Cash Machine: ACBC plywood; paint white with dark blue letters and arrows as shown, cut slots 1/2" x 4"

Rates Board: ACBC plywood; paint with erasable chalkboard paint, Trim: white, "rates" sign with dark blue letters.

Drive thru: Glazing: Plexiglas with 6" hole cut-out at bottom

Shutters: ACBC plywood, swing inside; paint white; magnet catch with dark blue lettering "closed today"

Cash drawer: paint white, cabinet pull

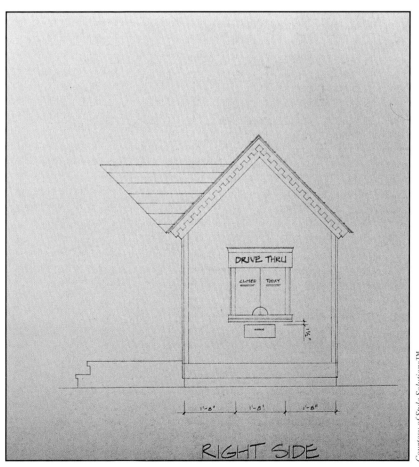

RIGHT SIDE

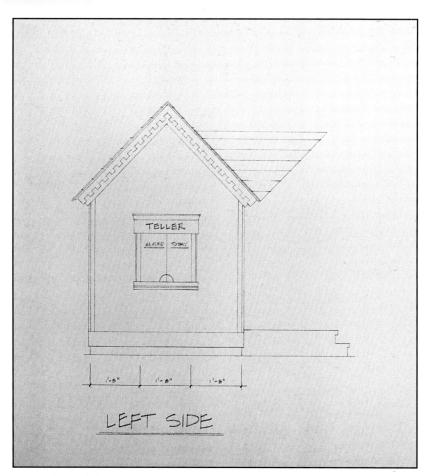

LEFT SIDE

Courtesy of Style Solutions™

Note: "Anti-Pinch Blocks" are 3/4" block on which shutter hinges are mounted to hold shutters off the wall and ¾" blocks at the sides of the drawer both inside and out to hold drawer faces off the wall so it cannot completely shut on a finger. The drawer is 11" deep so it can be opened from inside or out to pass money through.

Also cut door opening in plywood interior walls smaller than the door by 2" to create a 1" finger guard at the door hinges and a doorstop and head.

Teller Window: same as drive thru.

Safe: Add blocking between floor joists as shown, dashed to support a flush trap door in floor, hinges and pull should be flush with floor; ½" plywood bottom, screw on

Shutters: ¾" ACBC plywood, paint white, lettering dark blue; magnet catch.

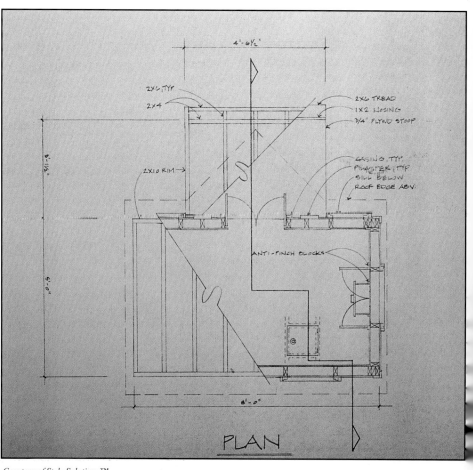

PLAN

Courtesy of Style Solutions™

A small cafe

Roof: Georgia-Pacific Summit Series shingles, color Desert Shake

Finials: Style Solutions™ Pedestal Ball B3X5; paint gold

Pineapple ornament: Style Solutions™ "Pineapple" PH5X9; paint gold

Fascia: Style Solutions™ Silhouette Moulding MLD620; paint cream

Front Door Mantel: Style Solutions™ peaked sunburst PSWDH28X14, paint cream with dark teal letters

Door and window casing and cornerboards: 1x3; paint cream

Door and window glazing: clear Plexiglas; paint dark teal lettering

Muntins: ½" applied wood or plastic trim; paint

Courtesy of Style Solutions™

Courtesy of Style Solutions™

cream

Door: ¾" ACBC Exterior plywood; paint cream, cabinet pull, magnet catch

Window Mantel: Style Solutions™ Florentine trim moulding MLD600, mount on Style Solutions™ flat trim FLT153, top with crosshead trim strip MLD602 and miter top edge; paint gold.

Window panel at front: Style Solutions™ window panel WDP37X18; at sides Style Solutions™ window panel WDP23X18; paint cream. Mount panels directly to studs, add Jack studs as necessary.

Window sill: Style Solutions™ cornice moulding MLD240; paint cream

Shutters: ¾" ACBC plywood exterior, Mount on exterior trim; paint cream, with dark teal lettering, round cabinet knobs, expose hinges, magnet catch

Siding: Georgia-Pacific ACBC SS ½" plywood; paint aqua, cut to leave ¾" anti-pinch guards at window and door hinges, (see plan)

Interior walls and ceiling: same as siding, decorative painting.

Courtesy of Style Solutions™

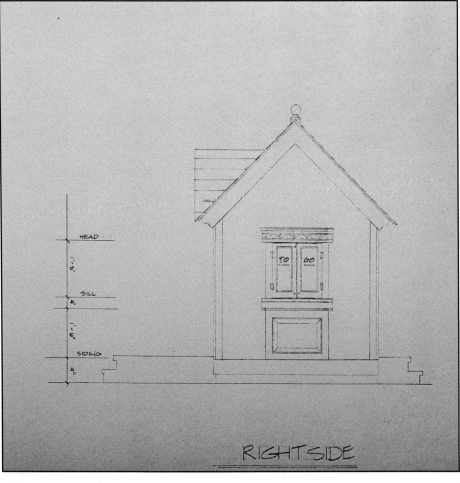

Menu Board: ½" SS ACBC plywood; paint with erasable chalkboard paint, letter the word "Menu" in dark teal color

Bell: Mount a ring-able bell on panel next to back door

Trash: Mount a plywood swinging door on 1x3 trim using a piano hinge; paint trim cream, board aqua, lettering teal

Trash can: any plastic trash can of size similar to shown: 17" wide x 11" deep x 24" tall, set next to swinging door

Back door: ¾" plywood, swing in; paint cream, clear Plexiglas windows with muntin trim

Back door mantel: Style Solutions™ flat trim FLT153-12; paint cream with teal lettering, crosshead trim strip: MLD602, (miter) corners.

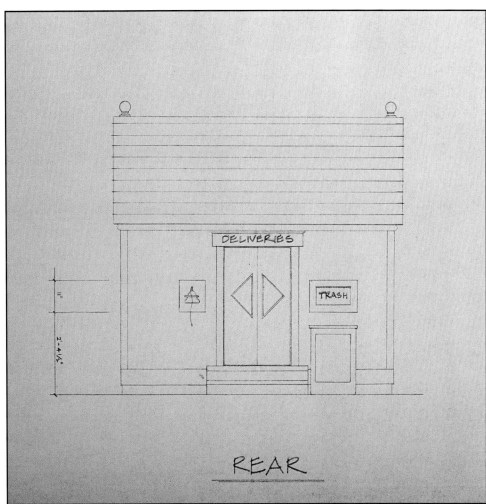

REAR

Courtesy of Style Solutions™

LEFT SIDE

Courtesy of Style Solutions™

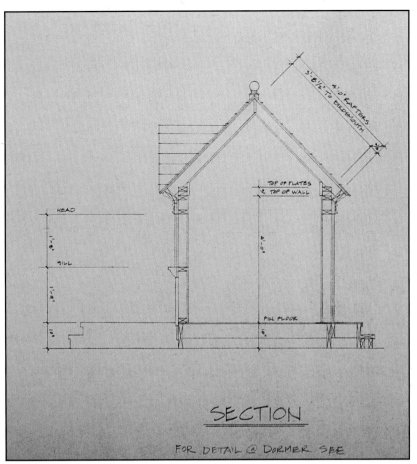

SECTION

FOR DETAIL @ DORMER SEE

Floor Joists: 2x6 at on center +/-, pressure
  treated
Rim Joists: 2x10 pressure treated
Floor: ¾" ACBC plywood; paint aqua
Studs, plates, and rafters: 2x4
Roof deck: ½" exterior grade plywood
Ridgeboards: 2x6
Cornerboards: 1x3; paint cream
Skirt: 1x6; paint aqua
Interior ceiling moulding: 1x6
Stoops: ¾" exterior plywood; paint aqua

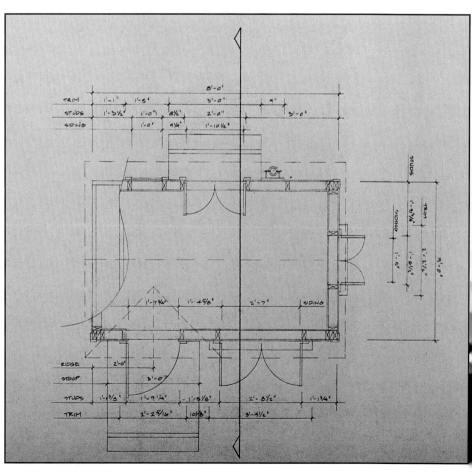

A small town hall

Chalkboard: Style Solutions™ Wall Niche NCH18x30; paint with erasable chalkboard paint inside, outside trim lavender

Roof: Summit Series Dove Grey

Steeple: ACBC plywood paint white

Fascia: Style Solutions™ chair rail MLD611; paint dark purple

Opening trim: Style Solutions™ Window Moulding MLDWM180, Lavender

Fascia: 2x6 paint lavender; and Style Solutions™ egg-and-dart trim MLD561; paint dark purple

Window mantels: Style Solutions™ MLD226, Miter top edge; paint lavender, lettering on right side dark purple

Window trim: Style Solutions™ MLDWM 180

Cornerboards: 1x2 paint lavender

Skirt: 1x6 paint dark purple

Stoop and Floor: ¾" ACBC plywood exterior grade; paint dark purple

Siding: Georgia-Pacific T1-11 with grooves 4" on center; paint white, (optional: cover channels with battens)

Front door trim: Style Solutions™ half-round spoked window pediment HRSP24X12; paint dark purple; 5½" Flat arch moulding Style Solutions™ AR24X6F; paint lavender with dark purple lettering; Rosette: Style Solutions™ Plinth Block PB5X5; paint lavender; Casing: Style Solutions™ MLD210; paint lavender

Front door: ACBC plywood; paint dark purple; Panel trim: Style Solutions™ chair rail MLD611; paint dark purple; clear Plexiglas door glazing; cabinet pull handle; cabinet pull, magnet catch

Courtesy of Style Solutions™

Courtesy of Style Solutions™

Courtesy of Style Solutions™

Courtesy of Style Solutions™

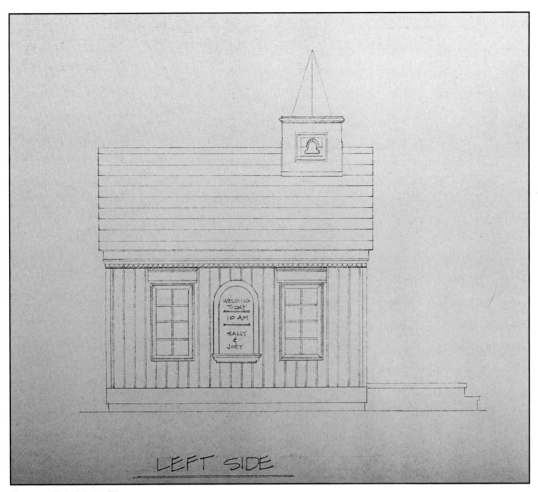

LEFT SIDE

FRONT

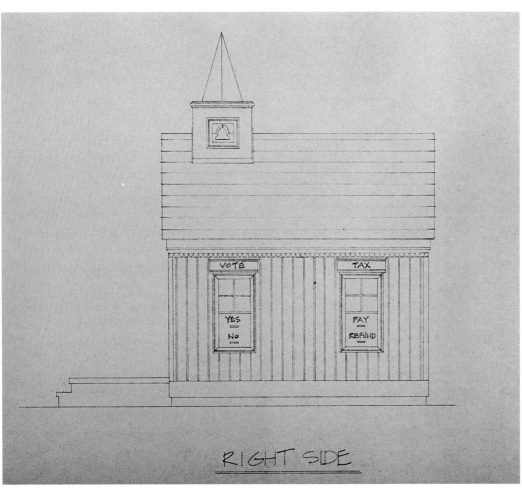

RIGHT SIDE

Rear windows: Two vinyl half-round windows; paint purple; remove glass and substitute colored Plexiglas in alternating pink and clear

Arched trim: (2) Style Solutions™ 5-1/2" flat arch mouldings AR24X6F; paint lavender with dark purple lettering, the state motto of Maryland or equal; paint stars gold.

Right side windows: Custom Plexiglas with applied muntins as shown on top only; paint lettering on Plexiglas dark purple, cut slots in Plexiglas.

REAR

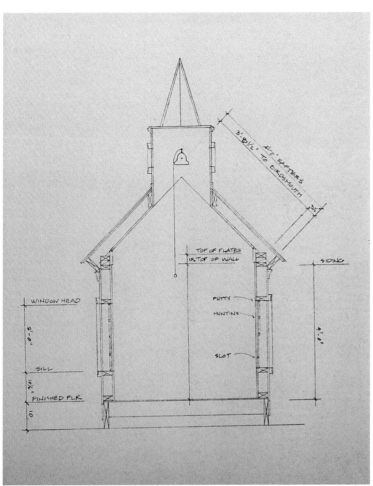

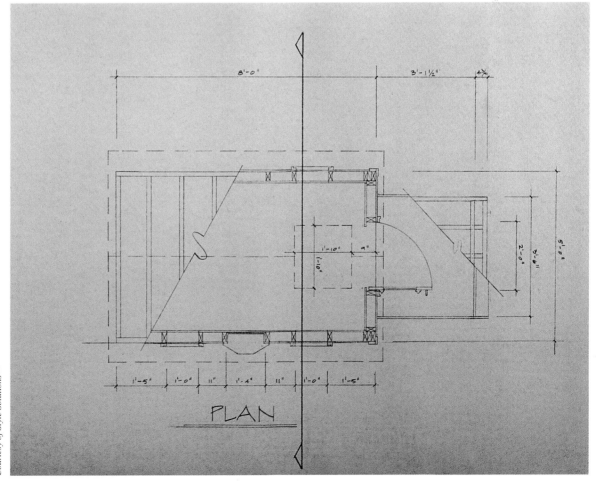

PLAN

33

A cottage for little ones

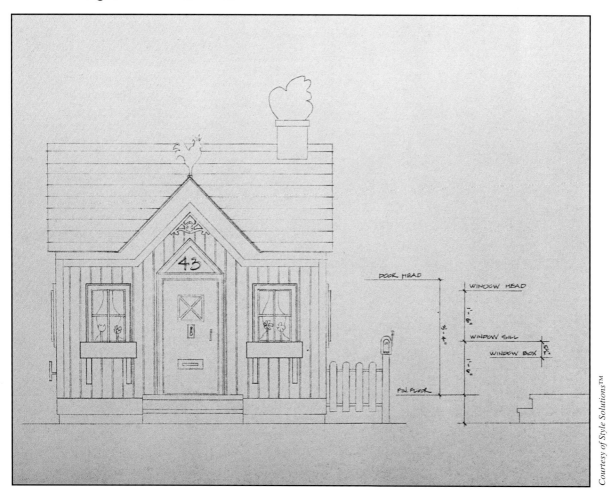

Courtesy of Style Solutions™

Roof: Georgia-Pacific "Summit Series" color Woodland Green

Chimney: ACBC 1/2" plywood; paint light green

Smoke: paint gray

Weathercock: paint crimson

Sparrow: paint brown

Flowers: paint bright colors

Door and window casing: Style Solutions™ MLDWM180; paint yellow

Fence: 1x3; paint white, space pickets at 2-3/8" max

Mailbox: use a real mailbox with flag

Door mail slot and knocker: use real ones

Front door: 3/4" ACBC plywood; paint bright yellow, magnet catch, cabinet pull, window and door and pediment glazing: clear Plexiglas, paint "43", Dark green

Siding: Georgia-Pacific ply-bead plywood; paint light green

Fascia: 1x6, 1x8 at dormer; paint dark green

Cornerboards and rake moulding: 1x3; paint bright yellow

Front bracket: Style Solutions™ "classic mini scroll bracket" BKT1OX12, take 2 brackets cut in half; use the smaller halves to make a whole small bracket, paint bright yellow

Side brackets: "take 4 brackets cut in half; use the larger halves to make 2 large brackets

Birdhouse: use a real wren house, unpainted cedar

Window boxes: 1x6, brackets: Style Solutions™ leaf bracket BKT7X9S; paint dark green

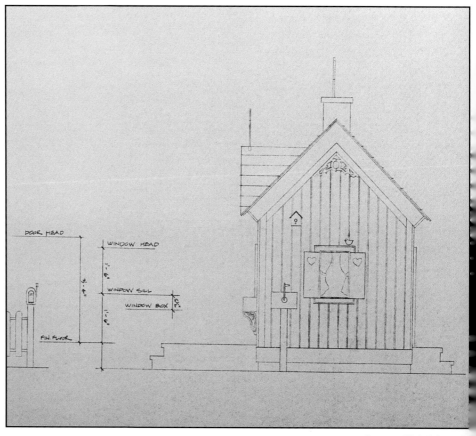

Courtesy of Style Solutions™

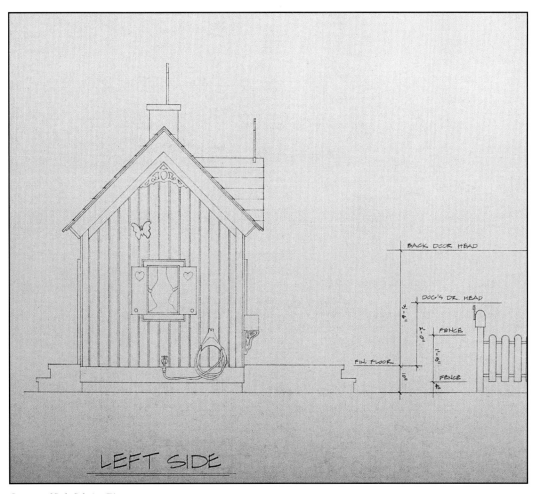

Atlas Moth: 1/2" ACBC plywood; paint brown

Hose Bib, plastic hose reel: purchased

Hoop: Purchased child-size plastic hoop, make a backboard to fit using ACBC 1/2" plywood; paint white

Shutters: 1/2" ACBC plywood, mount on exterior window casing with exposed hinges use wood cabinet knobs, paint shutters and knobs dark green, paint heart motif light green, magnet catches

Dog door and mouse door: 1/2" ACBC plywood, swing into house, wood cabinet knobs; paint doors and knobs bright yellow, paint names dark green, magnet catches

Door and window muntins: 1/2" wood or plastic trim; paint bright yellow

Note: Fencing may be continued to attach back at the other side of the house, enclosing a backyard accessed only through the house.

Curtains: staple lengths of bright yellow patterned fabric to inside window head, gather in, use the same-fabric for tie-backs

Skirt 1x6, paint dark green

LEFT SIDE

Courtesy of Style Solutions™

REAR

Courtesy of Style Solutions™

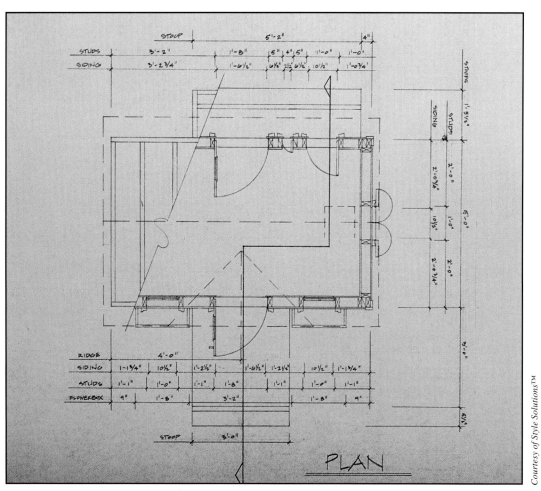

PLAN

Courtesy of Style Solutions™

Floor Joists: 2x6 at 12" on center +/-, pressure treated wood
Rim joists: 2x10 pressure treated
Floor: 3/4" ACBC plywood; paint dark green
(Stud Plates) Rafters: 2x4
Roof deck: 1/2" exterior grade plywood
Ridgeboards: 2x6
Interior ceiling moulding: 1x6
Stoops: 3/4" exterior grade plywood; paint dark green

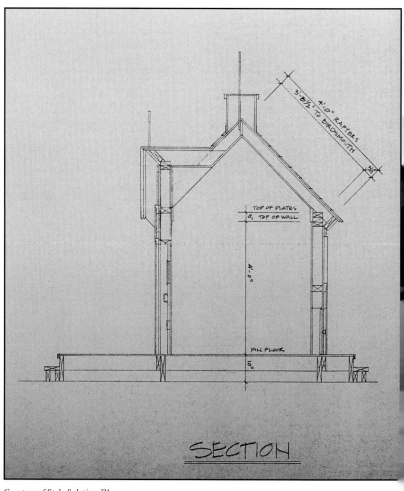

SECTION

Courtesy of Style Solutions™

Firefighters in training

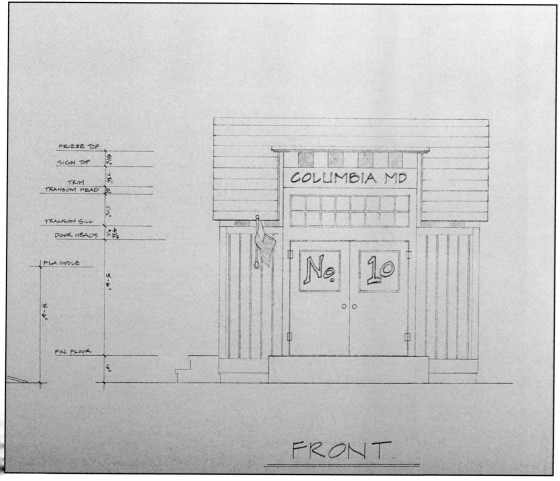

FRONT

Roof: Georgia-Pacific "Summit Series" Color: Antique Black

Fascia: 2x6; paint black and white glossy checks as shown with each square 5-½" x 5-½"

Siding: Georgia-Pacific T1-11 Rough surface 4" on center, Channel Groove paint high-gloss red

Corner boards and all trim: 1x3; paint high-gloss white

Signboard: 1x8; paint high-gloss white with black lettering

Doors: ¾" ACBC exterior-grade plywood; paint high-gloss white

Door and transom glazing: Clear Plexiglas, paint lettering black

Muntins: ½" wood or plastic trim; paint gloss white; no astragal moulding at double doors or shutters

Knobs: wood cabinet pulls; paint gloss white, magnet catches

Skirt: 1x6; paint black

Ramp, stoop, and floor: ¾" ACBC plywood exterior grade; paint black

Bell: purchased

Flag and mount: purchased

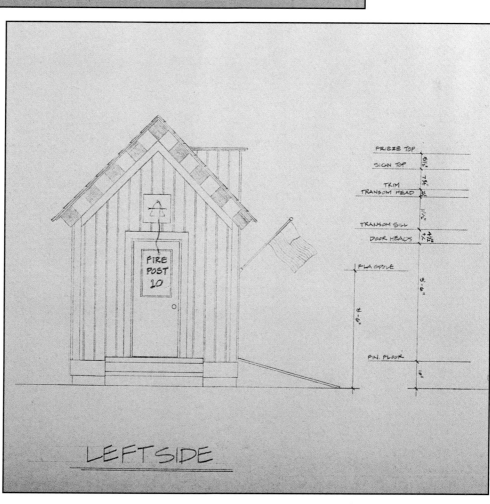

LEFTSIDE

REAR

Shutters: ¾" ACBC plywood, exterior grade; paint high gloss white; hinge to window trim

First aid sign: ½" ACBC plywood, exterior grade; paint red for cross with black lettering

Hose bibs, hoses, and plastic hose reels: purchased

Notice sign: ½" x 8" x 2' 7-½" ACBC plywood; paint high-gloss white with black lettering

Notice Board: ½" ACBC plywood, exterior grade; paint with erasable chalkboard paint

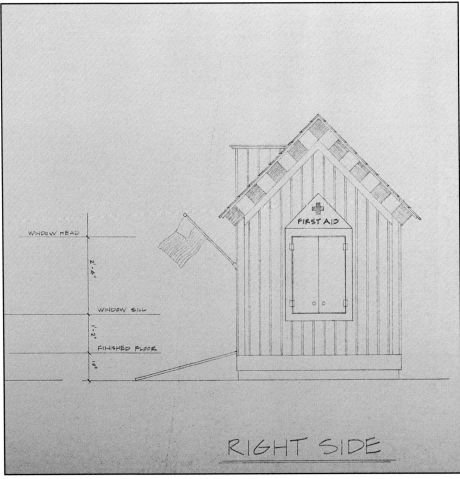

RIGHT SIDE

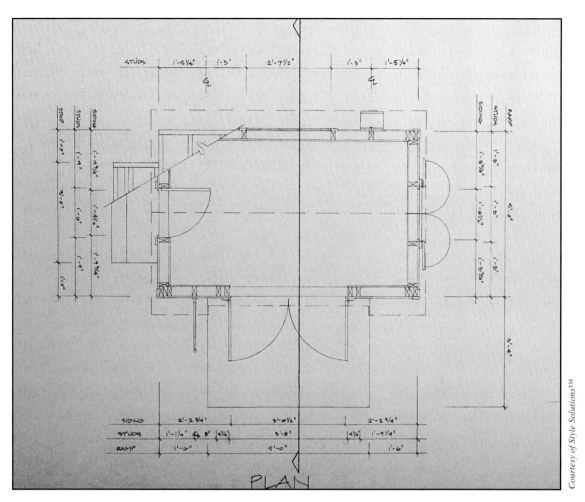

Floor Joists: 2x6 at 12" on center +/-, pressure treated
Rim joists: 2x10 pressure treated wood
Floor: ¾" ACBC plywood; paint black
Studs, plates, and rafters: 2x4
Roof deck: ½" exterior grade plywood
Ridgeboards: 1x6
Interior ceiling moulding: 1x6
Stoop and ramp: ¾" ACBC plywood; paint black

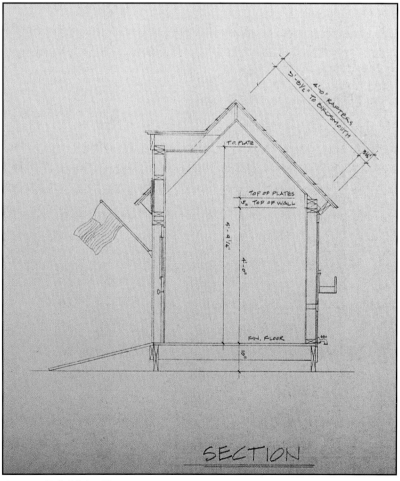

Do-It-Yourself

Starter projects for someone who wants to create
their own backyard play place

All the world's a stage

This playhouse is literally a stage for a "play," or the curtains can be drawn and it is an enclosed tearoom, a hospital ward, or whatever else a child might wish to imagine. The structure was designed by Alla Kazovsky, principal of Kids' Studio in Los Angeles. A mother and architect, Alla designs interiors, including furnishings, that provide tools for a child's work of exploration and growth. Her children's rooms are special retreats that acknowledge and celebrate individuality.

This playhouse was designed with all manor of play in mind. Planters allow children to start their own flower boxes or vegetable gardens, a sand pit is ready for digging in, and a curtain is ready to unfold on as yet unimagined dramas. The house can be made one or two stories high, and a swing arm can be built out the back for additional recreation.

Courtesy of Kids' Studio

Materials

Lumber

Quantity	Size	Length	To Make
6	2x4 treated	12'	Base, pressure
25	2x4 seams, overhang,	12'	Frame, roof roof "collar"
1	4x4	15'	Support beam
1	4x4	7-8'	Swing arm
12	1x4 construction grade	8'	Door and trim,
11 linear ft	1x2		Door stop
36 linear ft	1"		Trellises, sheathing

4 sheets of 3/4" x 4' x 8' plywood for playhouse floor and stage, sandbox, flower boxes, and trim along straight edges of base frame

8-10 sheets, depending on your skill, of T-111 grooved plywood siding
for roof and exterior

1 sheet 1/8" x 4' x 8' Masonite to trim curved edge of stage

Note:
• *If you don't have a table saw, have wood cut at the lumberyard.*

Fasteners
(Use galvanized fasteners whenever possible to prevent rust.)
8 3/8"x5-1/2" hex bolts
Box of #6 x 2" drywall/deck screws
30 3/8" x 3-1/2" lag screws
30 3/8" flat washers
Box of #10 x 4" drywall/deck screws
Box of #10 x 1-1/4" wood screws
Staples for screen door
Small nails for door stop and trellises

Hardware
1 half-base bracket to connect 4x4 post with 4x4 beam
1 doorknob
2 2-1/2" loose-pin hinges for door
2 5/8"x48" wood dowels for curtain rods
4 spring-clamp devices (often used to hang brooms) to hold curtain
dowels
8 grommets for canopies
8 hooks to fasten grommet-edged canopies in place
2 3/8"x4" threaded bolts, each with washer and locknut and nylon bush-
ing, to hang swing

Tools
Hammer
Drill with screwdriver bits
Portable circular saw
Hand-held saw

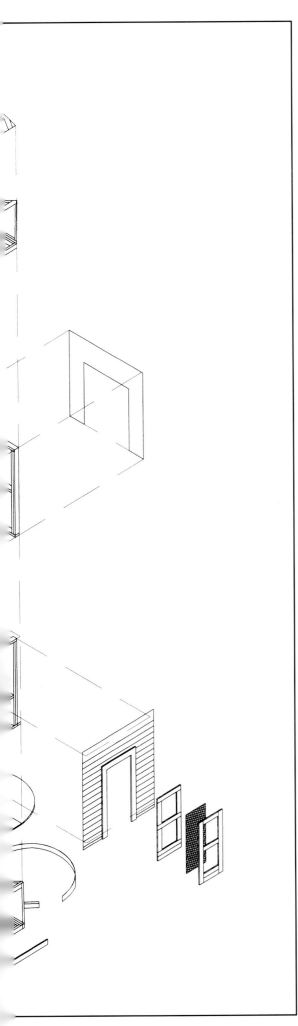

Clamps to use for door
Utility knife
1-3/8" hole saw to cut doorknob hole
Table saw
Adjustable wrench
Level
Chisel to mortise hinges
8-foot straightedge (or piece of wood)
Tape measure
T-square
File and sandpaper for smoothing

Miscellaneous
Small sack of concrete
Approximately 1-1/2" x 5' vinyl screening
Wood filler
Primer
Exterior latex semi-gloss paint in selected colors
6 yards x 57" wide fabric for stage curtains and canopies.
2 yards x 60" wide fabric to edge curtains
1" plastic rings for curtains
Polymer strap and 3/16" chains for swing

Notes:
- *Measure as you build and don't cut materials until you've verified your actual dimensions.*
- *Before sheathing, verify that framing is square by measuring diagonals. They should be equal.*
- *To avoid splitting wood, drill pilot holes before inserting screws*

Step 1: Assemble frames and cut out floors

Cut pressure-treated 2x4s and assemble according to plan to make the rectangular base frame for the house and the triangular base frame for the stage. The house frame measures 5' 10-1/2" x 5' 11-1/4". 2x4s are doubled on all four sides

Attach the triangular stage base to the house base with hex bolts as indicated.

Cut plywood and piece together the playhouse floor and the stage floor using a 2' 11-7/8" radius semicircle

Fasten on top of base frames with #6 x 2" drywall/deck screws

Cut two pieces of 3/4" plywood 6' x 4' each, and one piece 5' 10-1/2" x 4" to trim straight edges of base frame; fasten to frame with #6 x 2" drywall/ deck screws

Cut and piece Masonite to 9' 5-1/8" x 4" to trim curved edge of base frame. Fasten with #6 x 2" drywall/deck screws

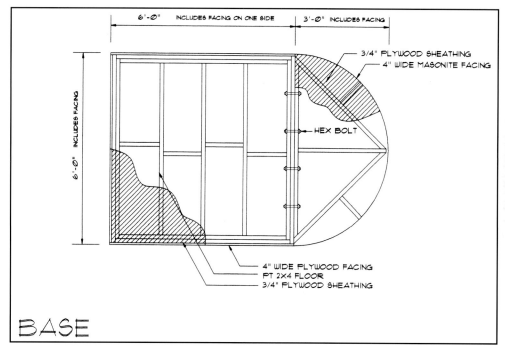

BASE

Courtesy of Kids' Studio

Step 2: Frame and assemble walls

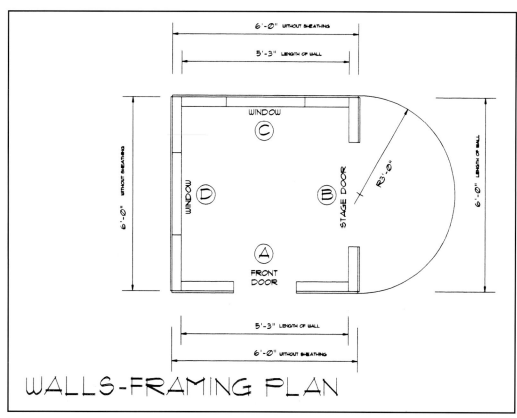

WALLS-FRAMING PLAN

Courtesy of Kids' Studio

Cut 2x4s according to plan and elevations, and frame the walls. Fasten walls to the base and then to one another using 3/8" x 3-1/2" lag screws and 3/8" flat washers

Front door wall A measures 5' 3"W x 6'H

Stage door wall B measures 6'W x 6'H

Window wall C overlooking sandbox measures 5' 3"W x 6'H

Window wall D overlooking swing measures 6'W x 6'H

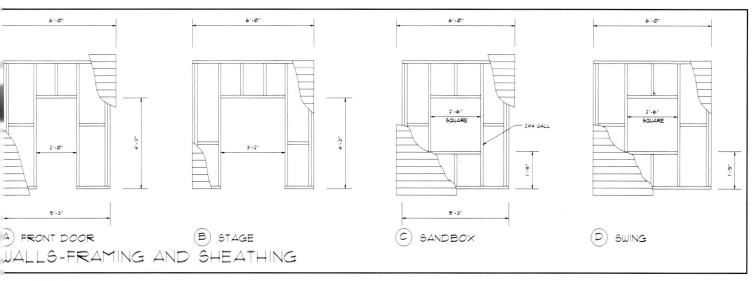

(A) FRONT DOOR   (B) STAGE   (C) SANDBOX   (D) SWING

WALLS-FRAMING AND SHEATHING

Step 3: Build overhang

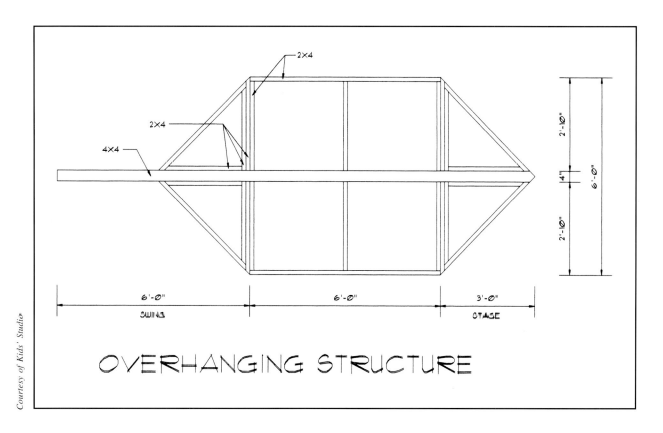

OVERHANGING STRUCTURE

A 4x4x15 beam runs horizontally overhead, anchoring triangular overhangs at either end

Fasten the beam securely to the swing wall and stage wall from below, up through the 2x4s, using a minimum of two #10 x 4" drywall/deck screws

Using #10 x 4" drywall/deck screws, fasten 2x4s to the top of walls B and D, aligning them with inner edges of the walls below, and fitting them between the 4x4 beam and the 2x4s fastened to walls A and C

Following the plan, cut 2x4s to make the triangular overhangs and fasten using #10 x 4" drywall/deck screws

On the swing side, a 4x4 vertical post rises about 6' 4" above ground and helps support the beam. The total length of the post depends on the slope of the ground and how deep it is buried. Dig a hole. Connect post to beam using the half-base bracket. To prevent deterioration, place the bottom of the post directly against the dirt {{{**is this correct???**}}}. Mix concrete as direct on package and pour it around the post, not underneath it.

Step 4: Make roof; Sheath exterior

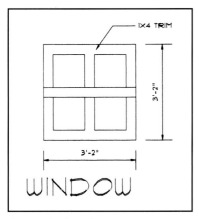

WINDOW

Cut 8 triangular panels from 5/8" grooved plywood siding, aligning vertical grooves before cutting so they line up when panels are joined at the center and to one another. This can be time consuming, but is important if you want a professionally finished appearance. Join panels in pairs, with a 2x4 behind the center seam attached from the front with staggered #6 x 2" drywall/deck screws. Join the four roof panels to one another with #6 x 2" drywall/deck screws, overlapping edges as in plan. To give the roof rigidity and support, make a "collar" of 2x4s, 3/4" away from the lower inside edge of the pyramid using #6 x 2" drywall/deck screws. Fasten roof to overhanging structure using #10 x 4" drywall/deck screws.

Sheath the outside of the structure with 5/8" plywood siding (grooves positioned horizontally). Following the elevations shown in Step 2, cut and piece the siding to fit around all openings. Before you cut, and again as you fasten siding to frame using #6 x 2" drywall/deck screws, carefully align the horizontal grooves of the siding. As with the roof panels, this can be time consuming, but this gives the playhouse a finished look. The inside walls of the playhouse are not sheathed; the frame of the structure shows.

Step 5: Apply trim

To trim openings around windows, front door, and stage opening, cut 1x4s and fasten over grooved plywood siding using #10 x 1-1/4" galvanized wood screws

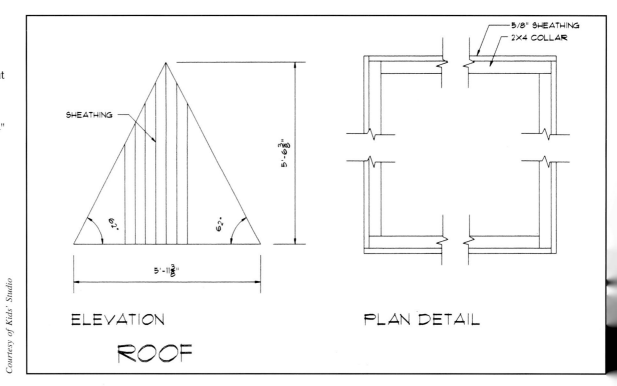

ELEVATION
ROOF

PLAN DETAIL

Step 6: Make door

Cut 1x4s into lengths as shown

On a sturdy surface position one layer of 1x4s without securing. (The finished door has vinyl screening sandwiched between two layers of 1x4s.)

Staple vinyl screening to top crosspiece of the door. Extend it past the bottom of the door and top with another layer of 1x4s. Working from top to bottom, using clamps as necessary, pull screening taut, staple it to 1x4s, and partially insert #10 x 1-1/4" wood screws. Gradually tighten all screws, checking that diagonal measurements are equal to ensure that door is square. Trim screening with utility knife.

Use hole saw to cut a hole in the door. Screw doorknob into place

Hang door with 2-1/2" loose-pin hinges. Cut 1x2s and nail around the door opening at top and sides so door can't swing through.

DOOR

Step 7: Build sandbox, flowerboxes

Make sandbox and flower boxes with 3/4" plywood assembled with #6 x
   2" drywall/dck screws
Sandbox bottom measures 5' 9-1/4" x 4' 1-1/4" x 4' 1-1/4"
Sandbox sides measure (1) 5' 10-3/4" x 12" and (2) 4' 2" x 12"
Cut two flower box bottoms, each measuring 1' 10-1/2"L x 6-1/2"W
Flower box sides measure (4) 6-1/2" x 12" and (4) 2' x 12"
Make trellises with 1x1s cut according to elevation and joined with small
   nails. Position a trellis in each flower box and fasten trellis to box from
   the outside with small nails.

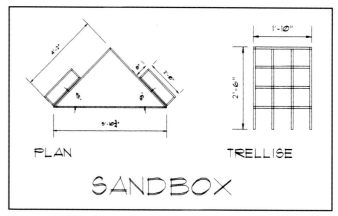

PLAN   TRELLISE

SANDBOX

Courtesy of Kids' Studio

Step 8: Prime and paint

Patch holes and seal seams with wood filler as necessary. Prime all surfaces
Apply two coats of exterior latex semi-gloss paint inside and out.

Step 9: Hang swing

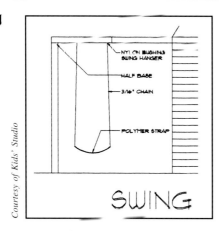

Courtesy of Kids' Studio

SWING

Attach swing hardware to overhead beam and
   hang polymer strap from 3/16" chains.

Step 10: Make curtains, canopies

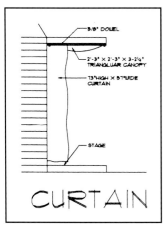

CURTAIN

Courtesy of Kids' Studio

Make two stage curtains, 73" high and 57" wide overall, allowing for seams and
   hems as necessary. Edge with contrasting binding if desired. Sew a row of plastic
   rings 1-1/2" below the top of curtain when it is hung. Thread rings onto dowels.
   Fasten a spring-clamp device along the bottom of each overhang, one at either
   end, to hold dowels in place.
Make two triangular canopies, each measuring 2' 3" x 2' 3" x 3' 2-1/4" overall. Attach
   grommets at each corner and midway along the longest side. Attach hooks in
   corresponding places inside the stage overhangs. Hang canopies from grommets

American Gothic

The following instructions and simple graphics wee designed to help even the most novice builder assemble a fantasy playhouse in the form of a fancy, Gothic chapel. Children will enjoy this as a great place to let their imaginations soar, and adults will enjoy the architectural ambience it adds to the back garden. It was provided courtesy of the Southern Pine Council.

This design includes 35 square feet of interior space (approximately 5' x 7') plus a two-foot wide porch across the front. The overall footprint is 5' x 9'. Provide at least 8 feet of open play area on all four sides. The spire requires a minimum clearance of 12 feet. Situate the playhouse on a level site, convenient for children to go to . . . often.

Inside the wall framing permits easy installation of shelves for all kinds of playthings. The height of this playhouse even permits a small loft at the rear. For furnishings, consider only movable items – light enough for the junior residents to rearrange, at will. Outside, attach a mailbox and street numerals for that "moved in" look.

•It is important to verify local building code requirements pertaining to setbacks, placement within a property, and/or any other restrictions before construction begins, and to obtain all necessary building permits from your local authority.

•Make sure you verify the location of utilities, both underground and overhead, before setting exact locations of posts.

• Refer to the materials list for required items. Depending on the location, exact size and finished details, slightly more or less of these items may be needed.

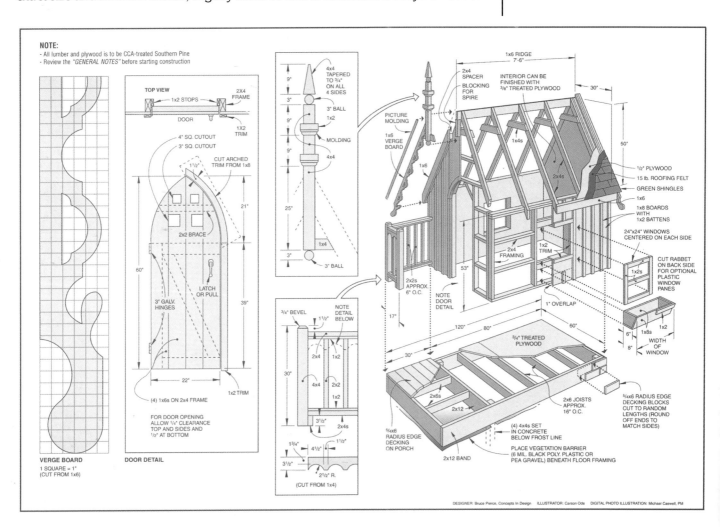

Materials

CCA-treated Southern Pine is recommended for all lumber and plywood material listed below. The 2x12 base framing and 4x4 posts are to be treated to .40 for Ground Contact. All other items can be treated to .25 Above Ground Use or .40 retention level.

Lumber

Quantity	Size	Length	To Make
3	2x12	10'	Base frame
5	2x6	10'	Joists
1	4x4	12'	Corner posts
3	5/4x6 (premium grade)	10'	Porch decking
7	5/4x6 base (standard grade)	10'	"Stones" around
26	1x8	10'	Siding, door trim
10	1x6	10'	Door, verge boards, fascia
2	1x4	10'	Door braces, trim, railing trim
30	1x2	8'	Battens, trim
8	2x2	8'	Spacers at roof, trim at windows
36	2x4	12'	Rafters, wall framing, railings

CCA-treated Plywood

Quantity	Size		To Make
2	4x8x3/4"		Floor
4	4x8x1/2"		Roof sheathing

Other Materials

15lb. roof felt, shingles, galvanized hinges, door latch, joist hangers
2 windows
Vegetation barrier (gravel or plastic)
All fasteners, connectors, and hardware should be hot-dipped galvanized or stainless steel. When construction is complete, an application of water-repellent sealer, paint, or stain is recommended.

Kiddy picnic table

Here is the perfect project when you are ready to furnish your fun house: the following picnic table is perfectly proportioned for big play. It's easy to assemble, and makes a great weekend project for a handy mom or dad. The plans were provided courtesy of the Southern Pine Council.

Courtesy of Southern Pine Council

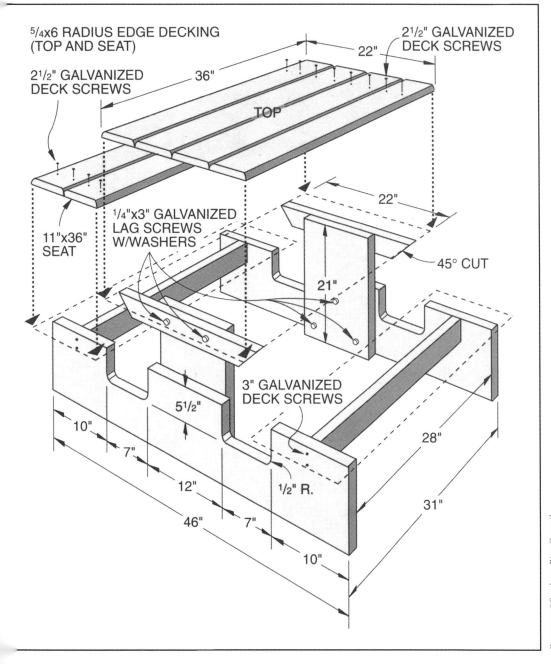

5/4x6 RADIUS EDGE DECKING (TOP AND SEAT)

2½" GALVANIZED DECK SCREWS

2½" GALVANIZED DECK SCREWS

22"

36"

TOP

11"x36" SEAT

¼"x3" GALVANIZED LAG SCREWS W/WASHERS

22"

45° CUT

21"

3" GALVANIZED DECK SCREWS

5½"

10"

7"

12"

46"

7"

1/2" R.

28"

31"

10"

Builder Profiles

Barbara Butler

San Francisco-based designer and builder Barbara Butler creates whimsical structures worthy of the most active imagination, and she's been well financed in her creative pursuits by Hollywood, design magazines, and a growing number of celebrity clientele across the country who are eager to own a piece of her work. Butler draws on her own childhood when fashioning play places. She has fond memories of a rope swing in an old tree, two metal bars at different heights, like chin-up bars, and a "three-foot-high rock wall around part of the house that we could pretend was a ledge next to a lava pit when we were learning to climb."

Imaginations can set up housekeeping in these colorful little kingdoms. Both homes feature a Dutch door and hinged windows that shed light interiors as creatively decorated as the exteriors. One was done in a mystical garden theme, the other a storybook theme with imaginative carving on all four sides: The front wall has birds, a butterfly, frogs, tulips, and a working mailbox; a Universe Wall has stars, a silvery moon, planets, comet, and a stargazing cat, an Underwater World wall has dolphins, fish, eel, seahorse, and lobster, and a Garden Wall has an apple tree with a monkey, squirrel, bird, and a friendly dog. Both play houses are 5' x 5' x 9'.

Photo by Teena Albert/Courtesy of Barbara Butler

In college she studied political science, but after graduation learned bricklaying and construction from an older brother, James, who was a contractor renovating houses on Capitol Hill. After an intermission in graduate school, she moved to San Francisco in 1983 and started building decks, hot tubs and fences as co-owner of a business called Outer Space Designs. A request for a play structure snowballed, and Butler now employs about thirteen people in her playhouse and furniture building business.

Coined the "Rough & Tumble Outpost," this was built to stand up to the constant play of the five kids who own it and all their friends. Three towers, two bridges, two slides, a "jail" with barred windows, a secret door, climbing walls, swinging bridge, crazy climb bars, swings, and a fire pole are among the amenities.

This magnificent tree fort is deep in a ravine. Perched high on top of a 9' tall tree stump it is inspirational. Step across the swinging bridge onto a full wraparound "look out" deck. A trap door from the upper deck leads to a small bridge, a "cross-over" to the rock climbing tower below. Here you can take the Turbo Tube Slide for a quick way down. Or, run back to the rear of the deck and escape down the 15' fire pole and disappear in the rock maze below.

This three-color scheme of ochre, forest green, and barn red were all achieved using natural, custom-mixed, tung-oil stains that also work to preserve the wood. The Atherton Castle features a small secret storage compartment, two swings, a tube slide, fire pole, stacking fort, rock climbing wall, flagpole, a bridge over two swings, shuttered lower windows, and a two-level fort with open verandah on top.

Photo by Teena Albert/Courtesy of Barbara Butler

Photo by Teena Albert/Courtesy of Barbara Butle

This color scheme is typical of artist Barbara Butler's work. She lets her inner child out when it comes to staining and adorning her play homes and activity centers. This unit was commissioned by Walt Disney for the film "Bicentennial Man," starring Robin Williams. It is complete in every detail, with three towers, a bridge over two swings, a swinging bridge, a rope climbing net, a turbo tube slide off the back (not pictured), a fire pole, a climbing ladder, and a rock climbing wall. Every kid's dream!

Oppositie page: The Robin Hood's Fort is designed to fit in a 24' x 24' space, which provides 6' of "run-around" play room on all four sides of the structure and fits more practical budgets and smaller yards. This two-story fort includes a front door with peephole and door knocker, a jail bar window on one side, shuttered window on the other side, fourteen small cut-out windows, a secret escape door out the back, a mail slot, a turbo tube slide off the back, a rock-climbing wall, a stainless steel fire pole with gate, and a flag pole with three flags.

The view is magnificent from this octagonal lighthouse perched high on the edge of the ocean. The copper roof is slowly developing a beautiful blue-green patina, reflecting the deep colors of the sea. Notice the exquisite colors and detail of the carved climbing poles. 4'8" x 5'6" x 10' high.

Photo by Barbara Butler /Courtesy of Barbara Butler

Custom Playhouses

Lynda Bontrager and her husband, Marvin, fell into the children's playhouse business naturally. A builder for many years, Marvin was inspired by a new grandchild to start creating homes in miniature. The Victorian Ashlynn, was the first in what would become a whole line of playhouses.

"He is very talented in being able to look at a house and recreate the style in miniature without any plans," says a proud wife and grandmother, Lynda. The whole family is proud, and involved, now. Their six children and a son-in-law and a daughter-in-law are all involved in different aspects of the business.

Like themselves, the Bontragers find that their customers are trying to offer their children or grandchildren a childhood dream that they once had. "The majority of our customers had a playhouse, or wished they had a playhouse, when they were little. Or else they had a friend who had one and they played in it," she said. "They want to recreate memories like that for their children.

All of their homes are scaled to accommodate adults standing up – that way the children don't outgrow them. Most of their playhouses are custom built, though they have started a line of Pre-Built Kits. These come in toddler size (4' x 4' x 5') and a size for toddlers to teens (6' x 6' x 7').

Painted to match their parent's home, this Dutch Colonial style playhouse (8' x 11' x 10') has a cedar shake roof, custom-crafted French windows, and Colonial pillars. Inside it has hardwood flooring, insulation, and a chair rail. But one of the features that most impressed its little occupants was a working doorbell. One of the favorite hangouts is the little loft over the porch with a peephole toward the parent's home in front.

Courtesy of Custom Playhouses

59

Courtesy of Custom Playhouses

This little home (8' x 11-1/2' x 10-1/2')is loaded with character, created with cedar siding, a handcrafted scalloped frieze, window boxes, and dormer windows jutting out from rustic shutters. All of the windows open and close, and the front door is a Dutch door. There's also a non-operational stone fireplace inside, and hardwood floors.

This little garden cottage (8' x 12' x 12') lends itself to creative paint jobs. Here the trim and the Victorian spindled porch are sprinkled with cheerful colors. Another pretty feature is a decorative adult-size door with leaded glass. The inside was furnished with a sunflower theme, complete with custom-made curtains.

This little girl's backyard has become a field of dreams. Her dream home includes her very own mailbox, a built-in kitchen with operating sink, a stone fireplace (just for pretend), and a ceiling fan. Outside, vinyl windows are decorated with scalloped trim and window boxes.

Courtesy of Custom Playhouses

Courtesy of Custom Playhouses

Courtesy of Custom Playhouses

62

This charming little cottage is characterized by handcrafted sidelights flanking the Dutch door, French windows with screens, and a roof cupola. The cupola was crafted, along with the porch railings and the porch light, to match mom and dad's home. When their children outgrow it, this structure is perfectly suited to be a garden shed.

Courtesy of Custom Playhouses

Courtesy of Custom Playhouses

This little girl was instantly charmed by her playhouse, a Victorian with fancy woodwork work in the trim and a nifty oval window in the loft and on the front door. Her home also has a working porch light and doorbell.

Absolutely gorgeous, this little Victorian (10' x 13' x 13') is huge on charm and detail. A handcrafted Victorian accent is the centerpiece, set in the front gable. Below, an oval window crowns a door complete with brass kick plate. The turret is topped by fish-scale panels over round-top windows. The pink and lavender color theme was maintained inside and out. And the inside was designed with electricity, cable, and a phone jack.

Courtesy of Custom Playhouses

Courtesy of Custom Playhouses

Courtesy of Custom Playhouses

Same style, but the paint job has changed. This house enjoys a commanding view from a hilltop.

Courtesy of Custom Playhouses

Here's a sweet little Victorian (8' x 8' x 10'), trimmed up in green. A bay window accommodates a comfy window seat in the front. Wood accents include inserts above the door, porch, and gables, spindles on the porch railing, and a pie ledge on the Dutch door.

Courtesy of Custom Playhouses

Designed for a little girl who loves yellow, this house was furnished with custom wainscot painting and chair rail, sweet lace curtains, and a yellow chenille sofa sleeper. Outside, a fish-scale covered cupola and handcrafted gable finials add flair to the roofline.

Courtesy of Custom Playhouses

This lakefront property (8' x 15' x 12-1/2') is perfect for play. It is powered by electricity for winter heating and an operational ceiling fan in the summer. In high Victorian style, the outside has been lavished with hand-crafted roofline frieze and finials and cresting for the roofline.

Courtesy of Custom Playhouses

71

This little house (6' x 6' x 7') arrives as panels ready to be assembled. It can be used inside or out, and was designed with toddlers in mind. The working windows and shutters are one of the features kids like best about the house.

Courtesy of Custom Playhouses

This is truly an all-weather playhouse because it was designed to be used indoors. Here it is installed in a doctor's office waiting room. The low doorway says "children only," and they can't resist a trip. Everything in this house is askew, though the 6' x 6' x 7' structure is easy to build from a panelized kit.

Courtesy of Custom Playhouses

Courtesy of Custom Playhouses

73

Here's a setting for fantasy play about olden days. Settlers, lumberjacks, mountain men, and cowgirls can climb the front porch and call this little (8' x 11' x 10') spread home. A trap door inside leads to a loft.

Courtesy of Custom Playhouses

Courtesy of Custom Playhouses

Courtesy of Custom Playhouses

Courtesy of Custom Playhouses

Daniel Boone would have felt right at home here. There's a fireplace (just for fun) and a hunting trophy hangs on the wall. Adirondack chairs are the perfect furnishings, and the loft getaway comes complete with a panoramic view through Plexiglas windows, and a trapdoor. Tongue and groove walls and ceiling complete the rustic atmosphere inside, while log siding provides the period-perfect look for play.

Courtesy of Custom Playhouses

This castle kit was designed for easy home (or in this case, school) assembly.
The doors and windows work, and toddlers love the scale of make-believe
possibilities.

Katelyn's Kastles

Randy Jones built a castle for his own little princess, his daughter Katelyn, and now they share ownership of the business. Jones builds one-of-a-kind houses from scraps of lumber, salvaged architectural details, and antiques. He interviews all of his young customers before he begins a project and custom-makes his houses to reflect their secret wishes and fantasies. He also delivers and installs the houses himself, largely because he can't resist being part of the delight and excitement that overcomes a household, sometimes a whole neighborhood, when his small homes arrive. He has become known as "the fort fairy," and laughs whenever he hears it. His homes are an expression of his artistic inclinations, and each installation is as important to him as a gallery opening.

Courtesy of Katelyn's Kastles

You have to cross a bridge to reach this forest fort. There are three levels for play here, from the entry level where the front porch (flanked by crib spindles and rail) commands the best view. Inside, one must climb a ladder to reach the lookout tower, a little cupola with fanciful windows and bedpost trim. Going down the stairs leads to a deck in back and access to the magical woods beyond. Several stained glass windows and a flowerbox were added for the little girl who will play here.

A great big sunflower characterizes Stella's new digs, which she shares with magical fairies. The home has been prettified by alternating natural wood balusters and fancifully painted ones that match the supports for the side entrance. Pretty stained glass windows open onto the porch, where a picnic table and bench accommodate lots of play pals.

Courtesy of Katelyn's Kastles

80

This proud owner gave up a corner of her garden for a fanciful shed, that doubles as a playhouse for children who visit frequently.

What child could resist a romp up this rope-railed ramp? A "Keep Out" sign is only meant as a deterrent to girls, since this fort was built for a lucky boy. It includes a secret escape hatch through the floor, as well as a ladder off the back porch. And there's a crow's nest, too, for keeping a lookout.

Unfortunately, it's hard to see this little playhouse, sequestered as it is amidst the trees and bushes. But that's just the way its little owner wanted it – steeped in privacy so the children could escape to a world of make-believe. The parents enjoy a fanciful roofline topped by an old silo vent for decoration, and the knowledge that their little ones are only a holler away.

The Selby children wanted a place where their friends could come for sleepovers. This rustic, two-story log cabin was rebuilt from an old horse stall located on site. It got a new tarpaper roof, an old barn door, and a balcony. Antique window frames add character and authenticity to this early 1900s playhouse.

This little home is open for imaginary business – refreshments for sale, boats for rent. Let the fantasy begin. An old porthole window adds to the ambiance, and two benches invite others to join in the game. The building was commissioned for a church playground.

Tucked between home and garage is one kid's castle, complete with a few antique signs to stimulate trade in imagination. The building honors a grandfather, who once ran a general store in the area.

A fancy picket fence turned upside down adorns the area under the eaves. Split driftwood logs frame the window underneath and there's a duck nesting on the roof.

Lilliput Play Homes

Like most playhouse builders, Steven Chernicky was inspired to his new career by a crop of little ones — a son and daughter who've been well housed!

He is perhaps the most diverse children's home developer out there today, with dozens of different playhouse designs to his credit. This is partly because he has been at it for so long, since 1989. It's also because he works so hard. An incredibly clever man, he designs his play structures using panels, which makes them a lot easier to transport, and easy to assemble on site. And he delivers anywhere. His reputation, coupled with demand from his customers, has taken his homes to both sides of the continent and many points in between. He accepts all challenges, from making fantasy structures based on a child's fondest wish (to be a fireman, a Ghostbuster, a princess, or a bait-and-tackle shop owner, etc.) to recreating the parents' home in miniature for the child. He'll keep a structure small and simple, or build a mansion complete with electricity and plumbing. Herein is an impressive portfolio of images from his work, really only a small sample of what he has accomplished.

The muses: Alyssa Chernicky outside her Victorian Mansion and Evan Chernicky on the steps of his playhouse.

Courtesy of Lilliput Play Homes

88

Courtesy of Lilliput Play Homes

Courtesy of Lilliput Play Homes

The Princess Cottage includes louvered shutters, a dormer with window, and door and window accents. A doorbell, skylight, hardwood floors, and a loft can all be added. Other options include wallpaper, interior wall stenciling and/or sponge painting. 8' x 5' x 7'3".

Courtesy of Lilliput Play Homes

Photograph by John Sanderson/Courtesy of Lilliput Play Homes

This playhouse was custom built to match the owner's home. The front door has a brass door knocker and handle with a lock to the right. The two-story home features a large bay window, wood paneling, and interior comforts such as carpeting and furnishings including a small sofa, a table, chairs, and a cupboard.

Courtesy of Lilliput Play Homes

A wrap-around porch allows for all-weather outdoor play, or you can enter through a pretty front door with four glass insets. Other amenities include four windows, interior stenciling, shelves, and a bookcase.

Courtesy of Lilliput Play Homes

The Storybook Bungalow includes a double-Dutch door, two window boxes, and shutters with heart decorations. An interior loft and skylight/vent can be added. Other options include a doorbell, simulated hardwood floors, and interior wall stenciling and/or sponge painting. 8' x 5' x 8'2".

Courtesy of Lilliput Play Homes

Photograph by John Sanderson/Courtesy of Lilliput Play Homes

Opposite page: This playhouse was custom built to resemble New Orleans-style architecture. The classic black and white facade is dressed up with colorful flags. Besides a beautiful arched entry door in front, there are French doors on the left side of the playhouse. The balcony is not accessible (per the customer's request). Two antique entrance lamps flank the front door.

Courtesy of Lilliput Play Homes

A blue and white playhouse with porch sits amid a bed of flowers. Two small chairs adorn the porch and add a touch of home. It is fully furnished with table and chairs, child-size cabinets, and a plastic refrigerator. The inside walls are papered with a white and blue pattern, and stairs lead up to a loft area.

Courtesy of Lilliput Play Homes

Courtesy of Lilliput Play Homes

Courtesy of Lilliput Play Homes

The Cotton Candy Manor is decked out in Colonial-style trim, with a sunburst window over the door. An interior loft leads to an exterior balcony. This playhouse can be customized to include a doorbell, skylight and/or vent, doorknocker, simulated hardwood floors, and interior wall stenciling and/or sponge painting. The columns supporting the balcony are 5' x 6", and the overall height is 9'6".

Courtesy of Lilliput Play Homes

Courtesy of Lilliput Play Homes

This Cotton Candy Manor was customized to include a gorgeous porch of hardwood with lattice concealing the base.

Courtesy of Lilliput Play Homes

Courtesy of Lilliput Play Homes

This house is very similar to the Cotton Candy Manor except that it does not have the balcony or the side extension. Nevertheless, it's picture perfect in spring and winter!

Courtesy of Lilliput Play Homes

This spectacular playhouse is truly amazing! It features six rooms on two floors, a stair tower, first floor deck, second floor balcony, indoor sandbox, carpeting, skylights, a doorbell, sponge painted walls, and hardwood floors. Outside there is a spiral slide and a 10' straight slide from the second-floor balcony. A matching swing set is also included. Overall it is 24' wide x 28' deep x 11' high.

Courtesy of Lilliput Play Homes

Courtesy of Lilliput Play Homes

Courtesy of Lilliput Play Home

Welcome to Candyland! This brightly colored home radiates fun. There is a skylight in the roof and a multi-colored deck behind the playhouse.

Inside this spectacular playhouse are two rooms and a loft. Large Palladian windows, a classic pediment and a small fan light over the front door, dormers, and arcades supported by columns. A small balcony connects to a ladder and slide. A tire swing and large bouncing ball hang from the balcony. Two bench trunks sit on the raised platform under the balcony.

Courtesy of Lilliput Play Homes

Courtesy of Lilliput Play Homes

Courtesy of Lilliput Play Homes

103

Courtesy of Lilliput Play Homes

For the budding politician, here's City Hall, a two-story playhouse with built-in columns to impress any approacher. Double doors with brass handles open to display an interior staircase, a shelf, two chairs, and a table.

Courtesy of Lilliput Play Homes

The J&R Saloon is straight out of the old west, complete with swinging doors and kerosene lanterns, and furnished with a wooden "bar," table, and chairs. In case a brawl breaks out, there's a personalized sign hanging out front to indicate who's the boss.

Courtesy of Lilliput Play Homes

Courtesy of Lilliput Play Homes

105

Courtesy of Lilliput Play Homes

This playhouse was custom made and functions as both playhouse and shed, complete with wide barn doors and lots of storage area. Outside, a patio holds stacks of lumber that form a tunnel. The balcony door leads to the upstairs room. A yellow slide and wooden ladder provide access to the balcony.

Courtesy of Lilliput Play Homes

Opposite page: For the little fisherman, this customized playhouse offers the perfect opportunity for a start-up venture. A ready made shop, it has a large display window and fishing nets and poles hanging on the inside walls.

COVENTRY ROD AND REEL

LIVE BAIT · TACKLE · TOURS

BAIT

In the workshop ready to relocate to its wee owner's home, this set-up is complete with gas pumps, office, and garage. Store hours are posted on the front door, and inside the boss has two rooms and a customer counter and table.

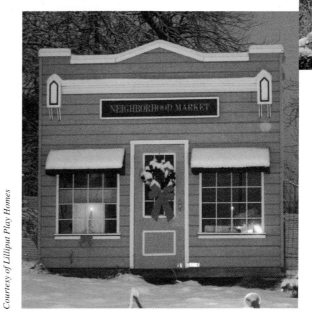

Any child can open their own neighborhood market. This start-up kit includes fabric awnings over the large display windows, Victorian accent trim, a personalized store sign, check-out counter, shelves, and display case. This playhouse can be customized into a Doctor's Office, Ice Cream Shop, Library, etc. 8' long x 5' deep x 6'10".

This colonial style playhouse has a large balconied entry porch with four columns. Inside, a staircase winds up to the balcony allowing access to the roof. There are five windows on the front of the house, three of which have louvered shutters. 44 square feet with a 24-square-foot porch.

The "master" house defines the Colonial Revival style of architecture with its large entry porch, louvered shutters, and square window panes.

This is a smaller version of the Westmoreland Regional Hospital in Greensburgh, Pennsylvania, and was presented to the hospital as a gift during a ceremony honoring the children who reside there. The 112 square-foot playhouse sees plenty of use.

The original Westmoreland Regional.

This playhouse is a miniature version of the Sewickley Academy; a private school in Sewickley, Pennsylvania. The architecture is reminiscent of Roman Classicism with its smooth columns and square base. The stucco exterior finish was painted red and white. The interior is furnished like a one-room schoolhouse. 64 square feet with a 16 square foot porch.

The original Sewickley Academy.

Done in the Swiss chalet-style of the parents' home, this playhouse includes interior columns, casement windows, fireplace, hardwood floors, and a skylight. The furnishings include a table and chairs under a loft which holds two chairs and a bed. On the far left is a garage door that opens to an area where the children can store their bikes. A doorbell and mailbox complete this adorable house. 100 square feet.

This is the "real" house, an impressive Swiss chalet-style home that was recently built for the parents.

Courtesy of Lilliput Play Homes

This "dream playhouse" reflects the architectural components found in the Queen Anne Style of American architecture. Fish-scale shingles line the projected roof, which overhangs three little window boxes full of flowers. Above the fully furnished, wrap-around porch is a tower with conical roof and three windows. Victorian trim lines the exterior. Inside, the stairs lead to a loft door that opens up to a slide. Hardwood floors run the length of the house, meeting a faux fireplace at the far left end. Complete with doorbell and brass door knocker. 92 square feet with a 31 square foot loft and 20 square foot porch.

Courtesy of Lilliput Play Homes

The main house.

Courtesy of Lilliput Play Homes

This little mansion sits atop a hill overlooking a tennis court. White French doors with brass handles welcome all inside, where three rooms including a loft allow for plenty of play. A love seat is surrounded by windows. 135 square feet with a 20 square foot loft.

Courtesy of Lilliput Play Homes

The parents' magnificent pink palace.

Courtesy of Lilliput Play Homes

This playhouse features fish scale shingles, a stained glass window, lattice underpinnings, Palladian windows, and window boxes. Inside, there are two rooms and a loft that leads to the balcony. Shown in two color variations.

Courtesy of Lilliput Play Homes

Photograph by John Sanderson/Courtesy of Lilliput Play Homes

The Victorian Mansion features a stained glass window over the front door, Victorian corbels, roof rails and window accents, cedar shingles, and an interior shelf. This playhouse can be customized to include interior wall stenciling or sponge painting, a doorbell, skylight and/or vent, and simulated hardwood floors. 8' long x 5' deep, with a 7' 6" tower and 6' roof.

Courtesy of Lilliput Play Homes

Built to suit any little mischief maker, this two-story hideout includes an upstairs turret with an opening just large enough for a water gun, accessed via an inside ladder.

Courtesy of Lilliput Play Homes

This tree house has a rope net along the left side for climbing. A slide sits next to a rope-and-ladder entrance. To the right are two swings and handlebars, which hang from monkey bars. The swings and handlebars can be detached so the monkey bars can be accessed. Underneath the "hide-out" there is an area that could be used for storing water pistols, sports equipment, and other fun stuff.

This white and green playhouse is similar to the previous treehouse. Two swings hang from overhead monkey bars. A picnic area lies beneath a balcony. The slide is in the back instead of off to the side.

Courtesy of Lilliput Play Homes

A beautiful little treehouse and picnic area, this design was color coordinated to match the customer's house. The 5 x 5-foot tower has a 10' swing beam.

Designed to accommodate a brother and sister, there is a classic fort upstairs for the little outdoors guy. Notice the signs, "No Girlz Aloud" and "Keep Out." A ladder, leading to the upper room, connects to a small balcony. Downstairs is space designed for a little girl who wanted to set up housekeeping. The structure measures 5' x 5', with a 10' swingbeam.

Fantasy

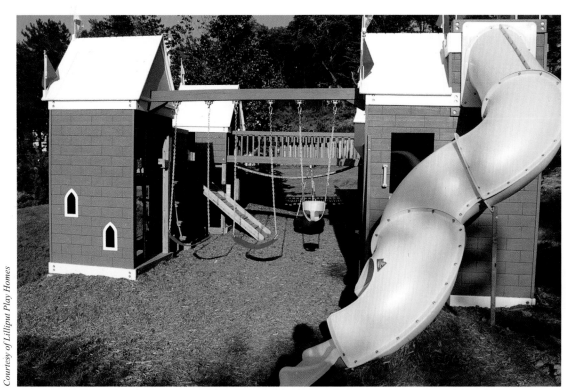

This fortress of fun includes wooden walls made to look like block, steeple-shaped windows, a drawbridge, and even a secret room which is accessed by a false wall panel. There are three swings, a rope to climb, a swinging bridge, a tire swing, climbing ramp, and a covered slide which wraps around to the side of the castle. A yellow tunnel connects the two towers in back. 12' x 20' x 12'.

Courtesy of Lilliput Play Homes

This white and pale peach castle sits alongside a small creek and a field of flowers. It was built for a special show at Phipps Conservatory in Pittsburgh, Pennsylvania. After it was photographed in the conservatory it was relocated to the Children's Museum of New Jersey in Paramus. Decorative and mystical with stucco finish and a stained glass window, it adds a little make believe to the world around it. Size: 12' x 12'.

The Riverboat Bed can be customized for any child. Exhausting play here can be taking a turn above deck manning the sailor's wheel. A mattress fits nicely below deck.

Courtesy of Lilliput Play Homes

This play firehouse is all ready for rescue vehicles to burst out the large "truck" doors. A second story can be quickly exited via a fire pole. 8' long x 5' deep x 8'2" high.

Courtesy of Lilliput Play Homes

This playhouse was built to resemble the Ghostbusters office, located in an old firehouse. Inside is a fire pole kids can slide down, and the station is wired for electricity.

Courtesy of Lilliput Play Homes

The Nickelodeon Theater has a stylish art deco design with a ticket window, a lighted changeable marquee, simulated neon lights, and seating on steps and the balcony. It is made all the more plush by carpeted floors, interior sponge painting and a window with shelves. 7' long x 5' deep x 7'2" high.

Courtesy of Lilliput Play Homes

This little red and white barn is ready to play farm. Two large barn doors on the front and side of the house allow easy access to what's inside. A loft holds toys and tools, while bikes and other large objects can be stored below. This barn is great for both storage and play.

Courtesy of Lilliput Play Homes

Another farmer's paradise, this play structure includes a silo with slide and a loft inside.

Little Mansions, Ltd.

    Stephen Pannell was always fascinated by small and beautiful in his artistic building pursuits. As a child he worked on models and made his own dollhouses. When his first niece came along, she was the lucky recipient of his first attempt at children's playhouse creation. The attempt went so well he decided to market them, and set out to create miniatures of some of the world's favorite classical homes. The beautiful structures are both fun for the children and folly for their parent's garden. His architecturally correct re-creations have been featured in *House Beautiful* and *House & Garden* magazines, and he has been called upon by several celebrities to deliver his hand-crafted creations to their homes.

Courtesy of Little Mansions, Ltd.

This Italianate Villa playhouse features wide overhanging bracketed eaves, arched windows, quoins, and a tower. All windows and doors are operable through the use of a 19th century styled key. The interior is L-shaped with plenty of room to play. Around back is a large "adult door" for the bigger folks. This playhouse is a little piece of Italy in the backyard! Exterior measurements: 8' wide x 10' long.

This Gothic style playhouse features simulated iron cresting atop the roof, pointed Gothic windows, steep gables, and authentic colors. An image of times gone by, this playhouse has an L-shaped interior, six working windows, and ample room for a small table and chairs. Exterior measurements: 8' wide x 10' long x 11' tall.

143

The Greek Revival. Built to suit any child, this playhouse is Greek architecture at its most fun. Four columns line the front and make for an awe-inspiring sight. The small child-size door opens with a 19th Century styled key; an adult door is in the back. Interior dimensions are 5' x 7' x 7' with plenty of room to play.

The Gothic Cottage is simple yet gorgeous in design and structure, displaying the charm of 19th century architecture. Features include working windows, decorative doorknobs, and flower boxes. This proud owner has landscaped with windmills, a giant candle, and neat white fencing.

Courtesy of Little Mansions, Ltd.

147

Storybook Playhouses

Matt Ward took his experience as a carpenter and builder and kept it all when he started making children's playhouses. He makes sure his playhouses meet or exceed construction and safety standards set by the home-building industry. All his homes include tongue-in-groove hardwood floors, handcrafted doors and windows, fully finished interiors, complete electrical wiring, clapboard siding, double-hung, insulated glass windows, and 25-year architectural shingles, among other things. And his homes are custom built, with options like built-in bookshelves, stenciling, insulation, doorbells, skylights, heating and air conditoning, and wiring for phones, computers, and an intercom system.

This beautiful display of Victorian architecture is picture perfect in yellow, pink, purple, and red. Features include hardwood floors (stained, varnished and stenciled with sunflowers), a hand-crafted arched door, interior loft with stairs, shutters, window boxes, keyed lockset, insulated glass windows, and electrical wiring. Inside, Victorian print wallpaper adds a touch of elegance to the playhouse.

Courtesy of Storybook Playhouses

Courtesy of Storybook Playhouses

Courtesy of Storybook Playhouses

Courtesy of Storybook Playhouses

Brilliant colors accentuate the architectural design of this Victorian playhouse. The porch banister is intricately carved to add character. The interior is painted pink and blue with wood accents. Built-in stairs lead to an interior loft.

Courtesy of Storybook Playhouses

153

Courtesy of Storybook Playhouses

With a brick base, exterior columns, and cherry wood door, this playhouse is a small scale "mansion." Window boxes decorate the windows in classic style. A sunburst window inset in the dormer above the entryway adds elegance to this already extravagant house. Inside, built-in bookshelves line the walls. Complete electrical wiring allows for phone, air conditioning, and stereo use. Hardwood floors and wood paneling touch up the interior.

Courtesy of Storybook Playhouses

Courtesy of Storybook Playhouses

Courtesy of Storybook Playhouses

This little Cape Cod was custom built for two little girls. It is complete with gable end jetty, cedar shake siding, and diamond-shaped and sunburst windows. The entryway is decorated with a heavy wooden door, antique wrought iron lanterns, a doorbell, and a mailbox. Inside, stairs lead to a bright loft. The walls are painted a sunny yellow with white trim.

Courtesy of Storybook Playhouses

Courtesy of Storybook Playhouses/Photos by Janet Lawson

Gorgeous pinks and grays accent the beautiful architecture of this gabled playhouse. An entryway dormer exhibits intricate latticework in pink. The interior is painted bright blue and green.

Courtesy of Storybook Playhouses/Photos by Janet Lawson

This quaint little cottage sits amid a forest of tall trees. Fish scale shingles and diamond window accent the entryway. Features include hardwood floors, electrical wiring, insulated glass windows and window boxes, and an interior loft with stairs.